M.N. OSUNA

Podcasting Pitfalls

A Beginner's Guide to Doing It Right

Contents

1

Hello

Hi, I'm Mo and I'm a podcaster. Unlike you, I had no idea what I was doing when I started. I've made every single mistake in this book. With that said, even with all my fumbles, I learned from my mistakes and managed to create a podcast that consistently sits in the top 15 of all medical podcasts in the United States (and it's always the top nursing related podcast in that category). So clearly, I've done some things right. But yes, I also did quite a few things wrong. In this book, I'll share the top 18 pitfalls podcasters fall into so you can start your show doing things right.

Ready to get started? Let's go.

2

Why Mistakes Matter in Podcasting

I f the thought of hitting "record" fills you with a surge of doubt, I've got good news, my friend. You are not alone. Podcasting is an incredible medium, but it's one that can feel like a giant ocean with a lot of unknowns murking about underneath. Mistakes are bound to happen, but my goal is for you to learn what those common mistakes are so you can avoid them right from the start. Will you make other mistakes? Probably. Actually, most definitely. But by then, you'll have your show built on a solid foundation and possess the experience and know-how to correct them.

Why focus so much on mistakes? It's simple. When you focus on what *not* to do, you save yourself time, money, and energy. You avoid frustration, poor listener experiences, bad reviews, and shows that fade out before they hit their groove. Think of this quick book as a friendly mentor who's been through it all and wants to make sure your experience is 1000x better.

Now comes the point in this book where you're wondering about my podcasting experience and how I can speak with authority on this topic.

No, I'm not a big name in podcasting. No, I don't have a podcast about podcasting. And no, I'm not trying to sell you on an expensive coaching program. I'm just a podcaster who loves what I do and wants you to love it, too!

My show is for a distinct audience, so there's a good chance it won't be your cup of tea. But if you'd like to check my bona-fides, you can look for *Straight A Nursing* on any podcast player. Give it a listen, read some reviews, and imagine your own show consistently getting this kind of positive listener feedback.

So whether you're a hobbyist who simply wants to talk about their passions, a business owner who wants to drive people into your sales funnels, or an influencer who wants to influence even more people, this guide is for you.

3

Planning Pitfalls

One of the biggest foundation mistakes you can make as a podcaster is not planning your show with intention. How do I know this? Because, like all mistakes in this book, I am guilty of this one big time! I honestly just started recording with absolutely zero plans in place and likely wasted a ton of time, money, and energy in the process. The only thing I had going for me was that I said things people wanted to hear. So at least I had that one part figured out. But with podcasting, there is so much more to consider.

There are three key pitfalls that fall under the planning category - not knowing your niche, not setting clear goals, and making your show overly complicated. Let's take a quick look at each one.

Pitfall #1: Not defining your niche

One of the biggest mistakes aspiring hosts make is trying to appeal to everyone. Without a niche, your podcast is likely to just blend into the background and not get noticed. Imagine you've just graduated medical school and are starting out with your first job as a resident. Looking for a way to brush up on key topics, you find yourself scrolling through dozens or even hundreds of shows. Would you rather listen to a show titled *"The Medical Show"* or *"The Medical Minute: Evidence-Based Tips for New Docs"*? The more specific you get, the easier it is for your target audience to find you, listen to you, and fall in love with you.

Action steps:

- Define your audience. I know you are probably chomping at the bit to hit record and JUST DO THIS THING ALREADY, but take a moment to define your niche. Who is your listener and what specific problems do you solve? If you don't solve a problem, what interests of theirs do you serve?

- Keep your ideal listener front and center. Write down your description of your ideal listener and attach it to your computer where you do your recording. Think of this person every single time you plan an episode and imagine you are talking directly to them when you hit record. When you find yourself straying off course, come back to this note and stick to your niche!

Pitfall #2: Not setting clear goals for your podcast

It's tempting to hit record and start talking, hoping that clarity will come with time. But without a defined purpose for your podcast, you're essentially wandering in the dark. Your overarching goal acts as your show's North Star, guiding every decision from content creation to marketing efforts. Are you here to educate a specific audience? Build a community around a shared interest? Inform about current events?

Advocate for a cause? Inspire positive change? Entertain people after a long day?

A podcast without goals is like a boat without a rudder floating aimlessly around a giant lake. Maybe you've listened to shows like this, though chances are you didn't listen for long. When a show doesn't have a clear goal, listeners don't know what they're going to gain from the experience, and typically have no clear motivation to return. This tends to happen when an enthusiastic podcaster hits "record" without defining the purpose of their show.

Here's another reason to set a clear goal for your podcast. When you know your show's ultimate aim, it becomes much easier to stay focused. If your goal is education, then every topic and guest should contribute to teaching your listeners something new. If it's building a community, you might prioritize listener interaction such as hosting Q&A sessions or streaming the recording live into a Facebook group where you can take questions in real time.

Without the clarity that comes with having a set goal for the show, your episodes risk feeling scattered, and listeners may struggle to understand why they should keep tuning in.

Action steps:

- Set an overarching goal. Begin by writing a simple goal statement for your show, something like: *"My podcast exists to [educate/enterta in/connect/inspire/inform] [specific audience or niche] about [core topic or theme]."* For example: *"My podcast exists to educate moms about creative activities they can do with their toddlers to boost readiness for school."* This statement ensures every decision you make regarding your show aligns with its ultimate purpose or goal.

- Set specific goals. Once you've defined your overarching goal, you can set more specific production goals that support that bigger vision, such as episode frequency.

Now that you've got your North Star in place, you'll find it easier to maintain consistency, create impactful content, and cultivate a loyal listener base that knows exactly why they should binge every single one of your episodes.

Pitfall #3: Making the show overly complicated

In a world with *a lot* of podcasts, trying to stand out can feel like an uphill battle. As of November 2024, there were an estimated 4.3 million shows worldwide, and industry trackers estimate that tens of thousands of new podcasts launch every month. That's a lot of voices vying for listeners' attention! In such a fiercely competitive environment, it might seem counter intuitive, but complexity often works against you.

New podcasters sometimes assume that packing their episodes with multiple segments, complex story arcs, and intricate editing tricks will help them rise above the noise. The result? Burnout, production delays, high production costs, and content that feels more chaotic than compelling. Instead of wowing new listeners, you risk overwhelming them (and yourself!) before you ever hit your stride.

A straightforward format is not only easier to produce, but also makes who you are and what you are offering obvious for your listeners. A simple structure keeps your show focused on your message, which is far more appealing to listeners than cool sound effects or gimmicks. Trust me, new listeners, who have a lot of other shows to sample, will appreciate not having to "figure out" your format before they can enjoy your show.

Action steps:

- Start small. Begin with the bare essentials and commit to this structure for your first 20 to 30 episodes. For example, a solo show could begin with a quick intro, a focused deep dive into one key topic, and a succinct sign-off.

- Write an intro and sign-off. Take some time now to write a quick intro and sign-off for your show. If you want to take this a step further, go ahead and record these elements (you know you want to!).

Pitfall #4: Not defining the show's structure

Jumping into your show without establishing a clear structure or format is like throwing a dinner party without deciding what's on the menu. Listeners appreciate knowing what to expect before they hit "play." A well-defined structure helps you stay organized, prepares guests (if you have them), and sets audience expectations. When listeners understand the show's format, they can settle in and engage fully rather than feeling disoriented or wasting time trying to figure things out. Plus, having a clear structure makes it easier for you to prepare episodes efficiently, ensure consistent pacing, and identify where changes are needed as you grow.

The most common podcast formats are:

- Solo show - In this style show, one host delivers the entire episode from start to finish. This is a great style of show if you are an expert in your field. It also has the benefit of being one of the easiest types of show to coordinate and edit.

- Conversational or co-host show - This type of show involves two to three co-hosts having a conversation about a particular topic. This type of show requires a substantial amount of editing and equal motivation from all parties.

- Interview show - An interview show involves the host bringing on a guest for each episode and asking them questions about a predetermined topic. It does require a bit of up-front work in that you must find potential guests, draft questions to ask them, and coordinate schedules. This type of show requires more technical expertise and many times guests do not have recording gear or stable internet connections, which can affect the quality of your show.

- Combination - Many shows thrive with a combination structure. Just be sure you do so with intention and not because your show lacks focus. For example, my show is a solo show though I occasionally do bring on guests for interviews.

Action steps:

- Decide on your show's structure before recording your first episode.

- If you plan to have a co-host or two, identify who these individuals will be. Confirm their interest and dedication to the show. It's also important to understand their availability for recordings and to divvy up tasks so the workload is equally shared.

- If you plan to have guests on your show, make a list of 20 individuals you would like to interview and start reaching out to them.

4

Technical Pitfalls

No matter how brilliant your ideas or how enthusiastic your delivery, poor technical execution can quickly erode a listener's confidence in your show. Crackling audio, inconsistent volume levels, or clumsy editing can make even the most compelling topics feel unprofessional and difficult to follow. Before you know it, a promising first impression turns into a frustrating experience that sends potential fans elsewhere. In this section, we'll look at common technical pitfalls that trip up new podcasters and explore simple solutions for producing crisp, clear, and polished episodes. We'll also discuss why your choice of podcasting host is a vital one right from the start. By mastering a few key skills and investing in the right tools, you'll ensure that your show's technical quality never distracts from the message you are sharing with the world.

Pitfall #5: Poor sound quality

My first 17 or so episodes are really difficult for me to listen to for a lot of reasons, but mainly because I had such a terrible microphone. I literally purchased the cheapest microphone I could find, which was a headset like telemarketers wear. While it was probably better than using the internal microphone on my Mac, it still didn't produce good sound.

Note that poor sound quality goes beyond a microphone that sounds less-than-great. Even excellent content can be overshadowed by static, echoes, muffled audio, and widely varying volume levels. And much of this work comes into play with your set-up, including where you record, how much sound absorption is in your environment, and the settings on your recording software.

Action steps:

- Invest in a decent microphone that fits your budget. Options that receive great reviews include Shure MV7, sE Electronics Neom, Blue Yeti, and Sontronics Podcast Pro (though, of course, there are many others).

- Choose a quiet recording space such as a small enclosed room. Even a carpeted closet works great due to the sound absorption qualities of the clothing.

- Purchase a pop filter or foam windscreen to reduce plosives and breath sounds.

- Add sound-absorbing elements to your space as needed. This can include heavy curtains, rugs, upholstered furniture, pillows, foam panels, blankets, or even a portable sound booth.

- Ensure fans, AC units, and noisy appliances are off when you record.

- Silence your phone (or better yet, place in Airplane mode), and silence any notifications that could come through your computer.

- Wear headphones while recording, which can help you catch unwanted sounds in real time.

- Do a test run! Record a short segment and then listen to it so you can make adjustments as needed.

Pitfall #6: Ignoring editing

While you may love the idea of off-the-cuff episodes, failing to edit your recordings at all can result in rambling content, mistakes, and bloopers. For example, I often teach pharmacology concepts so I have to say a lot of complicated drug names, which I rarely get right on the first try. Another reason to edit is to tighten up your show, improve the flow, and ensure you stay on topic. Your listeners have limited time and they'll drop off quickly if they have to wade through awkward pauses, unrelated tangents and filler words that don't add value.

Action steps:

- Decide if you're going to edit the show yourself or hire an editor. Both have their pros and cons, time and expense being the main ones.

- If you want to edit your show yourself, invest in editing software such as Audacity, Garage Band, Descript or Riverside. Then, take some time to play around and learn how to use it before you're in a time-crunch to get your first episode out the door.

Pitfall #7: Choosing the wrong host

Choosing the right podcasting hosting platform isn't just a minor detail or afterthought. It can actually have a big and lasting impact on the growth and management of your show. A poor choice early on could mean limited analytics, complicated workflows, and even difficulty appearing in the right podcast directories. On the other hand, a well-chosen host can streamline your process, deliver powerful analytical insights that shape your content, and help set you up for long-term success.

Of all the mistakes I made, I wish I had realized I'd chosen the wrong host much, much sooner. But as a beginner, I had no idea what to look for. My choice of host led to convoluted publishing workflows that overly complicated the entire process. Happily, I am now with a podcast network and utilize Megaphone as my hosting platform. I can tell you, without a doubt, the difference is night and day.

So what is a podcast hosting platform? This is the home base for your show. It's where your audio files live and it generates the RSS feed that allows apps like Apple Podcasts and Spotify to distribute your episodes. It's also where you'll get your show analytics and even add designated locations inside each show for advertisers to run ads.

Here's what to look for when choosing a hosting platform:

- Solid analytics – Growth depends on knowing what's working and what's not working so you can make data-driven decisions. Look for hosting services that provide details on things like downloads by episode, geographic location of listeners, listening platforms, and retention rates.

- A user-friendly interface - If the interface is difficult to use or glitchy, you're going to get frustrated every time you upload an episode. A good platform has an intuitive dashboard and clear instructions for setting up your show's details.

- Seamless distribution - Your host should make it easy to submit your show to the major directories such as Apple Podcasts and Spotify.

- Scalability - As your show grows, so will your needs. Choose a host that is able to handle increasing numbers of downloads without price hikes that cripple your budget or service interruptions that throttle your show.

- Support - This goes without saying, but choose a host that provides reliable customer support especially as you are starting out and will likely have a lot of questions.

- Monetization options - A good host will include features like dynamic ad insertion so you can make money on your show.

- Website integration - Choose a host that makes it easy to integrate your episode with your website. Some hosts even provide website hosting as well, making it a one-stop-shop!

Some popular options for hosting include Libsyn, Buzzsprout, Captivate, and Anchor.

Action steps:

- Do your research. Explore different hosting platforms such as those listed above.

- Tentatively commit. Once you've made your choice, sign up for a trial or start with a monthly plan just to be sure it's a good fit before you commit long-term.

- Dive in! During your trial period, make sure you get in there and explore. Upload a test episode, check out the dashboard, and see what analytics are provided.

5

Content Pitfalls

Your content—the heart and soul of your podcast—is what keeps listeners coming back episode after episode. Yet, even the most passionate hosts can fall into traps that leave their material feeling unfocused, uninspired, or downright dull. From rambling intros that test patience to neglecting the wants and needs of your audience, these missteps can slowly chip away at the connection you're trying to build. In this section, we'll identify common content-related mistakes and provide practical strategies for sharpening your focus, refining your storytelling, and making every episode resonate. With a bit of direction and intentionality, you can transform your content into the driving force that hooks new listeners and keeps loyal fans tuning in for more.

Pitfall #8: Inconsistent episodes

Of all the mistakes I made, this was definitely in my top three biggest blunders. Chances are, you've experienced this as a podcast listener more than once. There you are, enjoying your morning commute because you discovered a fantastic new show. You get in the car on Thursday morning, expecting a new episode but it's not there. A week passes, then two. By the time a new episode drops, you've already moved on to another podcast (one that actually has a consistent publishing schedule). This is exactly what will happen to *your* listeners if you aren't consistent right from the start. Sporadic releases frustrate listeners, erode trust, and ultimately stunt your show's growth.

In a crowded podcast marketplace, your audience has plenty of alternatives. When you show up reliably—whether that's once a week, every other week, or once a month—you reassure them that their time and attention are valued. Consistency builds credibility and lets your listeners form a habit: they know exactly when to expect new content and can look forward to it. Over time, these predictable releases foster loyalty, prompting listeners to incorporate your show into their regular routines, such as commuting, working out, or meal prepping.

Additionally, many podcast directories and apps tend to favor consistent, active shows. Regular posting can influence recommendation algorithms and improve visibility, making it easier for new listeners to discover your content.

Before committing to a posting frequency, take an honest look at your availability and resources. Producing a polished weekly show may sound ideal, but if you're juggling a full-time job, family responsibilities, or other creative pursuits, it might be unrealistic. Instead of rushing into an ambitious schedule and burning out, start small—maybe a new episode every two weeks—and then adjust once you find a comfortable production rhythm.

One thing to be mindful of is avoiding what I call the honeymoon phase. This is when a podcaster gets *so excited* about their show that they release several episodes just a few days apart with no discernable pattern. It almost looks as though they simply recorded on sporadic days in the first two weeks and released episodes as they created them. And of course they did! They were so excited to share their show with the world! But, what usually happens is that they can't maintain this level of frequency, episodes never get released on a schedule, and the podcaster never finds their rhythm. Can you guess what happens next? To keep this from happening to you, make consistency a priority right from the start.

Action steps:

- Commit with intention. Take a look at your schedule and decide what you can realistically commit to. Successful podcasting is a long game, so plan to be in it for the long term. This means looking at the next twelve months (at least!) and determining a release schedule that you can maintain consistently. Try starting with a more conservative schedule, such as one episode every two weeks. You can always reassess after a few months and increase frequency if your schedule allows. If it doesn't, then simply stick with what works. Consistency isn't about posting daily; it's about meeting whatever schedule you've promised to your audience and delivering quality episodes they'll return to again and again.

- Create a content calendar. Start by mapping out your next six to ten episodes in advance. This helps you avoid scrambling for topics at the last minute and provides a clear roadmap for planning, recording, and editing.

- Consider batch recording. This is when you record multiple episodes in one session. By doing so, you vastly improve your workflow, minimize setup time, and ensure you always have episodes "in the bank" so you can release on schedule. I completely changed my show's trajectory when I started incorporating batch recording and, honestly, there's no way I'd still be doing podcasting eight years later without it.

- Set deadlines, and stick to them! Treat your show like any other work project with firm due dates. Make sure you build in time for research, scripting (if applicable), coordinating with guests, recording, editing, and promotional tasks. The last thing you want to do is rush to create an episode the night before your scheduled release date.

- Be transparent. If you do need to adjust your podcasting schedule, let your listeners know. A quick announcement goes a long way toward maintaining trust and lets your listeners know you haven't disappeared from their lives.

- Have a backup plan. If time is tight, you may want to consider outsourcing some of your podcasting tasks. Hiring an editor or using automated editing tools can free you up to focus on content creation so you always maintain that consistent publishing schedule.

Pitfall #9: Not knowing your audience

Take a moment and think about your favorite podcast. Chances are, you feel like the host "gets" you. They understand your interests, struggles, or sense of humor. That's no accident. Shows that resonate deeply do so because the creators know exactly who they're talking to. On the flip side, if you try to appeal to everyone without understanding who's on the other end of those earbuds, you risk serving up episodes that feel disjointed, irrelevant, or forgettable.

When you know your audience, you gain a powerful compass that points you toward engaging topics, relevant guests, and the right tone. Your listeners feel seen, heard, and appreciated. This rapport builds trust, encourages loyalty, and makes listeners more likely to recommend your show to friends, rate it highly, or support you financially if that's your goal.

Without audience insight, even polished production and great guests can fall flat. Imagine talking in-depth about complex medical jargon to a general-interest audience or featuring a lot of guests who share tips for busy moms when your audience is mostly young men. Most will tune out and your show won't thrive. By understanding who you're speaking to, you can strike the perfect balance between being informative, entertaining, and accessible.

Action steps:

- Create a listener avatar. Envision your ideal listener in vivid detail. What's their age range? What are their interests, goals, and pain points? Are they juggling a busy family life or a rigorous academic schedule? This mental portrait helps you tailor your content so it feels personal and relevant. Write this short description down on a sticky note and attach it to your computer screen so you can see exactly who you are communicating with when you speak into the mic.

- Use analytics and surveys. Most podcast hosts offer basic audience analytics that include geographic locations of listeners and which platforms they utilize. If you publish on Spotify, you receive a yearly summary of your audience information that includes age range, what music they like, and other podcasts they listen to. Combine this data with surveys or polls on social media and email newsletters. Ask your listeners what they struggle with, what they love about your show, and what they'd like to learn next. Direct feedback is gold, but only if you utilize it to grow your show.

- Engage on social media and communities. Join online groups, forums, or social media platforms where your target audience hangs out. What questions are they asking? What trends do they follow? Engaging with your community in these spaces helps you stay current with their evolving interests. Just be mindful of any rules about self promotion in groups managed by others. You're not there to promote your show, you're there to learn about your audience.

- Ask for feedback. Once you start publishing, encourage listeners to leave comments, send emails, or post reviews. Their compliments highlight what's working, and their complaints or suggestions reveal areas for improvement. By openly welcoming and acting on feedback, you show respect for your audience's opinions and gain insights into how to better serve them. One great way to say this is, *"What's challenging you right now in [your topic area]? Shoot me a message or leave a review. Your feedback will help shape future episodes."*

- Don't be afraid to experiment. Not sure if your audience wants more solo episodes or interviews? Try both and measure the response, just be sure to do it with intention. Look at download numbers, listener retention, and feedback to refine your approach. Over time, patterns emerge and guide you toward the content that truly resonates.

- Speak to one person. When recording your show, think about the listener. They're usually listening solo which means you should speak to them as if they are just one person. For example, don't say *"I believe in each and every one of you."* Instead say, *"I believe in you."* See how much more impactful that is? By connecting in this way, you engage the listener and build a loyal fan because they know you are speaking directly to them.

Pitfall #10: Overly scripted or totally unscripted episodes

This one can be tough for new podcasters because, let's face it, there's a fine line between sounding polished and sounding stiff. Overly scripted podcasts can come across as robotic or inauthentic, while completely unscripted episodes risk becoming meandering, unfocused, repetitive, and unprofessional. Finding a balanced approach ensures that your show feels both high quality and approachable.

With an overly scripted show, when every word is predetermined, you run the risk of sounding like you're reading rather than conversing. And yes, even if yours is a solo show you are still having a conversation with the listener. If you read the script, it comes across as though you are talking *at* the listener, rather than speaking to them in an intimate one-on-one way. Reading straight from a script can strip away the warmth, personality, and spontaneity that make podcasts so appealing. Listeners select shows because they want in on the conversation, not because they want to sit through a rehearsed (and possibly boring) presentation.

With that said, there are definitely drawbacks to being totally unscripted as well. Hitting "record" without any plan can lead to long, directionless conversations that test your listeners' patience. Rambling intros, off-topic tangents, and filler words can make even the most interesting subject feel tedious. Without a roadmap, you risk confusing listeners about your episode's purpose, causing them to tune out before reaching the good stuff.

The sweet spot lies somewhere in between. Instead of writing out every word, consider using an outline or set of talking points to keep you on track. These guides help you maintain a logical flow, ensure you cover all key points, and reduce awkward silences while still allowing your natural voice and personality to shine through.

Action steps:

- Create an outline for your first episode using talking points. Simply jot down a few bullet points for each section and try to stay away from full sentences, which you might be tempted to read. This will help keep you focused while also allowing you to have a conversational and engaging tone.

- Practice practice practice. Set up time to run through a practice recording session with your first script. If you find yourself stumbling over words or having trouble phrasing things the way you envisioned, this is a sign to add a bit more detail to your outline. Add in those extra key words that will help keep you on track and practice again. When you can run through the entire outline with minimal fumbles, you are ready to hit record for real!

- Speak in a natural voice. The first few times you run through your outline you may notice you sound a bit uncomfortable or awkward. Don't worry, this fades with repeated practice. Listen back to your test recording and make note of sections where you sound rehearsed, stiff, or just plain weird. Re-record those sections making an effort to envision your avatar. Remember, you're talking to one person. How would you phrase this if you were sitting across from them at a coffee shop? Try again and keep at it until your test recording sounds like the real you. Also, occasional small imperfections such as short pauses or even an intermittent "um" or "ah" can actually make you sound more relatable. Just be aware if you are overusing filler words or pausing too long, which can make listeners uncomfortable or even make them wonder if the recording stopped.

- Edit with moderation. While you definitely want to remove lengthy digressions, repeated points, and overly long silences, make sure you leave in some personality and spontaneous moments. Listeners appreciate authenticity more than a flawlessly scripted monologue.

- Solicit feedback. Once you have your test episode complete, send the recording to a trusted friend or colleague and ask for their feedback on your delivery. Their perspective can help you fine-tune your approach before you publish.

Pitfall #11: The long and rambling intro

If you've listened to podcasts for any length of time, you've come across the long and rambling intro more than once. Your listeners pressed "play" for a reason. Maybe they're curious about your topic, excited to hear your guest, or interested in your unique insights. Nothing tests their patience faster than a long, meandering introduction that never quite gets to the heart of the episode. With so many podcasts competing for attention, listeners often decide within the first few minutes whether they'll stick around or move on. A drawn out intro can send them searching for a show that delivers value faster.

Studies suggest that audience drop-off is highest in the opening minutes of an episode. If you spend too long recapping your week, diving into unrelated tangents, chatting about random things with your cohost, or repeatedly restating what's coming up, you risk losing listeners before they ever reach the main content. A concise, purposeful intro reassures your audience that you respect their time and have something exciting coming their way.

Action steps:

- Consider starting with a short hook to instantly grab your listener's attention. This is a compelling statement, statistic, or short anecdote that piques curiosity.

- Provide a brief overview of the episode's main topic. If you are interviewing a guest, provide a brief highlight of this individual. The goal here is to let your audience know what they will get out of this episode.

- Keep it brief. Try to get into the meat of your show within the first two minutes. I remember listening to a 15-minute episode where it took the podcaster almost six minutes to get into the tips promised in the title. Do you think I followed this show? Spoiler alert - no, I did not.

Pitfall #12: Not practicing your interviewing skills

Interview-based podcasts can be a treasure trove of insights, personal stories, and dynamic conversations, but only if you handle them well. When a host lacks strong interviewing skills, even a fascinating guest can seem dull. Poor questioning techniques, constant interruptions, or failing to prepare all contribute to an unengaging, ineffective interview.

Some common interviewing pitfalls include:

- Lack of preparation. Showing up without researching your guest's background or recent work leads to shallow questions and missed opportunities. Your guest (and your audience) will sense if you're just winging it and you're likely to come across as inauthentic.

- Asking predictable or generic questions. *"Tell me about yourself"* might be okay as a warm-up, but relying solely on generic prompts can make the conversation sound canned. Listeners want fresh perspectives and specific details that reveal who your guest really is.

- Interrupting or overshadowing the guest. Cutting your guest off, constantly chiming in, or sharing lengthy personal anecdotes can turn what should be their spotlight into your monologue. Interviews should feel like a balanced exchange, with the focus on the guest's insights.

- Not listening actively. If you're so busy thinking about your next question that you stop listening to your guest's answers, you'll miss chances to dig deeper and your audience will notice. Active listening leads to more spontaneous follow-up questions that uncover the real gold in an interview.

Action steps:

- Do your homework. Spend time researching your guest's background, accomplishments, and interests. Reading their articles, watching their talks, or listening to their previous interviews will help you craft thoughtful, original questions.

- Plan your interview, but stay flexible, too! Prepare a list of topics or questions, but be ready to pivot if your guest says something intriguing. Following the conversation's natural flow often reveals richer, more meaningful stories.

- Ask open-ended, specific questions. Instead of *"Tell me about your career,"* try *"What was the most challenging part of transitioning from bedside nursing to a clinical educator role?"* Specific questions encourage detailed responses and keep listeners engaged.

- Be curious and practice active listening. Focus on your guest's words and tone. If they mention a surprising fact or an emotional moment, follow up. Your curiosity will guide the conversation toward more interesting territory.

- Stay self aware. Monitor how often you speak versus your guest. A good rule of thumb is letting your guest talk about 70 to 80% of the time. If you catch yourself rambling or interjecting with your own stories, take a moment to pause, and invite them to continue.

6

Marketing and Distribution Pitfalls

Y ou've poured your passion into each episode, refining topics, improving sound quality, and honing your delivery. Now comes the crucial step of getting those episodes into listeners' hands—or, rather, their ears. Marketing and distribution are the engines that drive discovery, growth, and engagement. Without a plan, even the best content can remain hidden, overshadowed by countless other shows. In this section, we'll look at common pitfalls—from assuming good content promotes itself to neglecting SEO—that can stall your podcast's momentum. By understanding these mistakes and learning how to avoid them, you'll give your show the best possible shot at standing out, connecting with the right audience, and building a loyal following over time.

Pitfall #13: "If you build it, they will come" mentality

It's a common fantasy shared by many new podcasters. You launch your show, upload a handful of insightful episodes, and simply wait for the downloads to roll in. But without active promotion, hoping listeners will magically find your show is like expecting customers to appear at a store hidden down a deserted alley, with no signs or directions. In today's crowded podcasting landscape, a strong marketing strategy isn't just a nice-to-have, it's a must.

With millions of podcasts available, even compelling content can languish in obscurity if no one knows it exists. Listeners rely on recommendations, social media posts, search results, and community discussions to discover new shows. Without a plan to get your name out there, you'll struggle to reach the people who'd genuinely enjoy and benefit from your episodes.

Action steps:

- Tap into existing social media communities. Choose one or two community platforms where your target audience hangs out and show up consistently. Keep in mind that most private community groups do not allow self promotion, so you'll need to be creative here. Be a regular contributor in your area of expertise and jump in the comments to help others out. When it feels appropriate, check in with the group moderators to ask them if it's okay for you to share an episode directly tied to the members' needs. Some community platforms to explore include LinkedIn, Facebook and subreddits.

- Start your own community. Another great idea is to start your own community such as a Facebook group. For example, if your podcast is about home organization and your target audience is moms, you could start a group called *"Busy Moms Get Organized"* and build a community full of potential listeners.

- Post on social media. Regular posting on social media platforms such as Threads, Instagram or LinkedIn is another way to promote your podcast. Note that these are posts shared from your account and are not part of private groups. When posting in this way, you are free to share whatever you like! Share episode highlights, behind-the-scenes snippets, and short audiograms to grab attention. Engage with followers by replying to comments, asking questions, and using relevant hashtags. When posting on social media, avoid being generic with posts like *"New episode is now live!"* Instead, work to grab the attention of your future listeners. For example, for an episode about time management you could say, *"Feel like there's never enough time in your day? In this week's episode, we dive into proven time management hacks that can help you get more done without the stress. Tune in now and discover how to take control of your schedule!"*

· Collaborate with others. Guest appearances on similar podcasts, blog post collaborations, and joint giveaways can help you tap into an established audience. Every strategic partnership exposes your show to potential new listeners who already trust the recommending source. More on this coming up!

· Optimize your metadata and SEO. Your episode titles, descriptions, and summaries should contain keywords that reflect what your audience is searching for. This way, podcast directories and search engines can showcase your show when someone looks up related topics. We'll dive deeper into this in an upcoming section.

· Build an email list. Build an email list from your website visitors or social media followers. With each new episode, send out a brief email or newsletter highlighting what's inside. Email marketing allows you to connect with interested listeners directly, without relying on algorithms or platform changes. Just make sure you follow industry standards for email list building so that your messages aren't considered spam. If you are interested in exploring this tactic, I highly recommend starting with the *Online Marketing Made Easy* podcast by Amy Porterfield. You can binge episodes related to email list building here: https://www.amyporterfield.com/category/list-building/

· Encourage listener engagement. Word-of-mouth can be especially powerful. Invite loyal listeners to share episodes with friends, leave ratings and reviews, or tag you on social media. When existing fans become ambassadors, your audience grows organically.

Pitfall #14: Not having a call to action

When I started my podcast, my only intention was to talk about the fascinating things I was learning as an ICU nurse. And while education in and of itself is a great goal for podcasting, I eventually turned my love of teaching into a business. Had I realized this at the time, I could have started building my email list and even monetizing my show much, much sooner. And I could have done that with a compelling call to action.

Imagine you've just delivered a fantastic episode, provided valuable insights, and maybe even taught your listeners how to solve a problem they've been experiencing. Now what? If you let the closing music roll without telling your listeners how to stay engaged, you're leaving a major opportunity on the table. A call to action (CTA) is your chance to guide listeners to take the next step. This could be as simple as asking them to follow the show, leave a review and rating, follow you on social media, subscribe to your email list, download a free resource, or check out your website.

The reason this is vitally important is that listeners are busy and easily distracted. They might love your content, but if you don't nudge them towards a specific action, they may never think to follow you on social media or opt in for that helpful free resource you've created. Over time, a well-placed CTA is what turns casual listeners into engaged fans and steady supporters of your brand.

Action steps:

- Decide on what your call to action will be for your first dozen episodes. Do you want to grow your email list or encourage people to follow the show? Whatever your goal is for these initial episodes, your listener can't help you achieve it without a compelling call to action.

- Write a short statement to use as your call to action. For example, *"If you enjoyed today's episode, hit the follow button so you never miss a show, and consider leaving a quick rating or review—it really helps us reach more people like you."*

Pitfall #15: Neglecting metadata and SEO

When it comes to podcast discovery, search engines and podcast directories play a bigger role than you might think. Whether someone's searching on Apple Podcasts, Spotify, or even Google, effective search engine optimization (SEO) and well-structured metadata help your show appear in the right searches. Ignoring these elements can mean missing out on listeners who are actively seeking the information, entertainment, or expertise you have to offer.

The truth is, many listeners don't find new podcasts by scrolling at random. They find them by searching for keywords that match their interests. If your show's title, description, and episode summaries fail to include those relevant terms, you're less likely to show up when they hit the search bar. Good metadata acts as your show's billboard, clearly stating what's inside so both directories and potential listeners understand its value.

Key elements to optimize as you create your show include:

- The show title. Make sure your show's title gives some hint about its content. For example, a show titled *"Running with Mo"* is broad and could be about any aspect of running. But if your show is about training for marathons, a title such as *"The Road to 26.2: Proven Tips for Marathon Training Success"* is far more targeted and will show up when a potential listener searches for the keywords "marathon" or "marathon training."

- Episode titles. Each episode title is another opportunity to be found. Instead of vague titles like *"Episode 3: A Conversation with John Smith,"* be specific: *"Time Management Hacks: Simple Ways to Reclaim Your Day with Productivity Pro John Smith."* This helps search engines—and listeners—quickly identify what they'll learn from that episode.

- Show description and episode summaries: Your show description and episode summaries should clearly state who the podcast is for, what topics you cover, and why it's worth listening to. Include relevant keywords in a natural way. For instance, if you produce a time management podcast aimed at busy professionals, terms like "productivity," "efficient routines," "goal achievement" or "work-life balance" belong in your descriptions.

- Tags and categories. Many hosting platforms allow you to choose categories or add tags. Pick the categories that best match your show's main theme and don't try to squeeze into categories that aren't relevant. Accurate categorization helps directories recommend your show to the right audience.

- Transcripts and show notes. While not always mandatory, providing detailed show notes or episode transcripts on your website can boost discoverability. Search engines can't "listen" to audio, but they can read text. By including a transcript, you help Google understand what each episode discusses which can help your podcast episode page rank higher in search results.

Action steps:

- Brainstorm keywords. Think about terms your ideal listener might type into a search bar. For example, if your show is about building resilience and managing stress, include phrases like "stress management tips" or "resilience strategies" in your metadata.

- Keep it authentic and natural sounding. Don't stuff your titles and descriptions with repetitive keywords. Listeners will notice this and it's another thing that can erode trust. Aim for natural language that flows well. A helpful, clear description will help your audience and search algorithms know what your show is about.

- Regularly review and update. Over time, your show may evolve.

Revisit your metadata periodically to ensure it still accurately represents your content and targets the right audience. If you expand from time management tips for new moms into broader productivity tactics for moms returning to the workplace, make sure your show's metadata reflects that shift.

· Test and track. Keep an eye on your download numbers and any analytics your hosting platform provides. If you notice a particular type of keyword or topic results in more listens, lean into that. Adjusting your metadata based on performance can help increase visibility.

· Rewrite. If you're already a few episodes into your podcast, go back and rewrite episode titles to include more descriptive terms. For example, *"Episode 10: Interview with Lisa Smith"* could become *"How to Master Meal Prep: An Interview with Vegan Nutrition Expert Lisa Smith."* Now, anyone searching for the keywords "meal prep" or "vegan nutrition" can more easily find your episode.

Pitfall #16: Neglecting cross-promotion opportunities

Even the best marketing strategy can stall if you're only preaching to the choir and relying solely on your existing audience and familiar channels. Cross promotion is about reaching beyond the boundaries of your current listener base and tapping into communities that share your show's interests and values. By getting in front of new audiences, you increase your show's visibility, grow your listener base, and build relationships with other creators and influencers in your niche.

Cross promotion works because people tend to trust recommendations from sources they already follow or admire. For example, when you appear as a guest on another podcast, you gain instant credibility from that host's audience. Likewise, partnering with bloggers, social media influencers, or online communities that align with your topic introduces you to listeners who are already engaged and interested. This approach can accelerate discovery. New fans are more likely to try your show because it's endorsed by someone they already know, like, and trust.

Action steps:

- Brainstorm guest appearance opportunities. Make a list of other podcasts that would be a good fit for cross promotion. For example, if your podcast is about training for a marathon, consider approaching the host of a show about running or sports nutrition.

- Consider shared episodes or feed swaps with closely related podcasts. This type of collaboration could include inserting a short trailer or snippet of each other's show at the end of an episode. Or, you could each agree to publish an entire episode of the other podcast on your feed. If you do this, it's best not to utilize it as your regular content as listeners might feel slighted if they don't get to hear from you. Instead, utilize this as a "bonus" episode on a different day of the week. Be sure to record an intro explaining why you love the show and encouraging your listeners to follow the other show (and, ideally, the host of the other show does the same for you!).

- Identify influencers and bloggers for cross promotion. Expand your promotion efforts outside of podcasting and identify bloggers, social media influencers, and YouTube creators who also speak to your target audience. You could offer to write a guest blog post, co-host a live chat, or collaborate on a short video series. By connecting with influencers who already have an established following in your niche, you gain exposure to an audience that's primed to appreciate you and your content.

- Network at local events and conferences. If your podcast topic lends itself to real-world events (expos, fairs, or professional conferences), consider attending and networking with other participants. Hand out business cards featuring your podcast, host a small Q&A session if appropriate, and forge relationships that could lead to interview opportunities, feed swaps, or joint marketing efforts.

- Automate the process. Create an email template you can use when pitching your show for cross promotion. Be aware that podcast hosts and influencers receive these pitches frequently and a message that isn't tailored to the show will very obviously stand out as "copy-and-paste." Use your template to guide the email, but make sure you do your research so you can personalize the message and authentically share the value you bring to *their* audience!

Pitfall #17: Poorly designed cover art

Your podcast's cover art is often the very first impression potential listeners have. Scrolling through a podcast directory, users see cover art before they even glance at titles or descriptions. If your artwork appears unprofessional, confusing, or irrelevant, many potential listeners might never click to learn more.

High-quality, eye-catching cover art suggests that you take your show seriously. It shows you've invested thought and effort into presenting yourself professionally. Clear, appealing visuals make your podcast seem more credible and inviting. On the other hand, sloppy, pixelated, or overly busy designs can send the message that the content is similarly disorganized or low-quality, no matter how great the show might be.

Elements of professional cover art include:

- Clarity - A clean, simple design that's easy to recognize, even as a small thumbnail. Too many elements can confuse rather than entice.

- Relevance - Visuals that reflect your podcast's theme, tone, or main subject. For example, a running podcast might use silhouettes of runners or an artsy image of a running shoe.

- On-brand aesthetics - Take the time to identify fonts, colors, and imagery that align with your show's personality and use these elements consistently.

- Readability - Your show's name should be legible at a glance. Avoid fancy fonts or cluttered layouts that obscure your title. Remember, most of the time this artwork is viewed as a very small image, so keep that in mind as you design this important graphic.

Action steps:

- Get inspired. Take some time to scroll through your podcast player app and notice which images catch your eye. See if you can identify what it is you find appealing and replicate that with your artwork. For example, is it a bold use of color, an engaging photo of the host, or a large and clear font?

- Hire a professional. Unless you have a background in graphic design, it's probably best to hire a professional to create your cover art. You can find affordable and talented designers through online platforms such as 99Designs and Fiverr.

- Get feedback. Once you have a few designs to choose from, solicit feedback from people you trust. If you have access to your target audience, create an online poll and seek their feedback, too. Not only does this ensure your show's cover art speaks to your potential listener, it can also get them excited for the release of your new show!

7

Long-term Pitfalls (AKA "Podfade")

L aunching a podcast is one thing. Sustaining it over the long haul is another. Many aspiring hosts start their shows with enthusiasm and ambition, only to find that podcasting is a *lot* harder than it looks. These hosts eventually find themselves struggling to keep up with production schedules, maintain consistent quality, and engage their audience as time goes on. Long-term pitfalls such as this can lead to what industry insiders call "podfade" which is the gradual slowing and eventual stopping of production.

Pitfall #18: Giving up because of long-term challenges

Statistics vary, but there's a well-known industry saying that many podcasts never make it past the seventh episode. Some research estimates that a large portion of new podcasts stall out before reaching the tenth episode. Buzzsprout, a popular hosting platform, has noted that while millions of podcasts exist, a significant percentage become inactive within their first year of launch.

This phenomenon, commonly referred to as "podfade," often occurs when hosts realize the demands of consistent production, topic research, editing, and promotion exceed their initial expectations. Without a sustainable plan, burnout is a very real possibility, and the once-exciting project can quietly fade into obscurity. When you experience these long-term pitfalls, it makes it that much easier to let your show fade away. If you want to be successful and have a podcast that sticks around, plan from the beginning how you'll avoid falling victim to these long-term pitfalls:

- Burnout from unrealistic expectations. New hosts sometimes enter podcasting with the idea that growth will be rapid and effortless. When the downloads don't skyrocket overnight, or production takes more time than expected, frustration sets in. Without adjusting expectations, celebrating small milestones, and focusing on gradual growth, it's easy to lose motivation.

- Ignoring listener feedback. A steady stream of episodes doesn't guarantee listener satisfaction. Over time, neglecting comments, reviews, and requests can alienate your audience. If your listeners don't feel heard, they may drift away, leaving you with stagnant download numbers and waning enthusiasm.

- Not evolving over time. Sticking rigidly to the same format, style, or topics for too long can cause your show to become stale. Successful podcasts grow with their audience. This can include introducing new segments, improving production quality, or exploring adjacent subject areas that capture listener interest.

- Lack of a sustainable workflow. This is probably the biggest factor of them all. Early on, it might seem easy to juggle recording, editing, and promoting all by yourself. But as episodes pile up, a lack of streamlined processes or support can lead to time crunches and stress. Without systems to keep you organized, the once-manageable workload can feel insurmountable.

Action steps:

- Set realistic goals: Instead of aiming for thousands of downloads per episode right from the start, focus on producing a consistent schedule of episodes with gradually improving quality. Celebrate progress, like reaching 10 episodes or your first 100 subscribers.

- Engage with your audience. Regularly ask for feedback and listen to what your audience has to say. Incorporate their questions or topic suggestions into future episodes. This ongoing dialogue fosters a sense of community and keeps your content relevant and evolving.

- Refresh your format periodically. Don't be afraid to experiment. Introduce a new segment, try a short Q&A portion, or invite guest experts. Keeping content fresh prevents both you and your listeners from losing interest over time. A great practice to incorporate is to regularly review your analytics to identify what's working. Is a particular episode type getting more downloads? Lean into that. Are listeners dropping off at the midway point? Tweak your pacing or segment structure.

- Build a support system. Consider outsourcing certain tasks such as editing or transcription so you can focus on content creation and strategic planning. Even simple automation tools, editorial calendars, or project management apps can help maintain a sustainable workflow.

· Batch your content. This was already mentioned in the chapter on content pitfalls but it bears repeating. Batching content is one of the most effective ways to maintain consistency and avoid podfade. The way I approach batch recording is I complete six episodes at a time. Because my show teaches complex nursing-related topics, this process does not occur in one day. It actually spans one to two weeks, depending on my other commitments. A show that's less time intensive to create could potentially be batched in a couple of days. Just make sure you create a workflow that matches your style of show and how much time and effort goes into each episode.

· Check in regularly. Make a point of checking in with yourself regularly so you can review what's working and what's not working. Small adjustments made regularly can keep your show on track and help prevent burnout.

8

Goodbye

B y now, you've taken a guided tour through some of the most common pitfalls facing new and even seasoned podcasters. From shaky planning and technical hiccups to marketing blind spots and long-term challenges, this book highlighted areas you need to strengthen or perhaps completely rethink. But rather than feeling daunted, I want this knowledge to energize and inspire you. As someone who has been where you are right now, I know what it feels like to take the leap into unfamiliar territory. My goal with writing this book was to help you start miles ahead of where I did so that you can grow your show faster, feel more joy in the process, and fulfill your dream of sharing your message with the world.

As you embark on this process, I want you to understand that no one starts out as a perfect podcaster. We all stumble, take wrong turns, and hit unexpected roadblocks. What sets successful, long-lasting shows apart is the willingness to adapt, improve, and keep showing up for their audience. Armed with the insights in these pages, you're already way ahead of the curve (and you're definitely way ahead of where I was when I started out!). By taking the time to understand where potential problems lie, you can hopefully avoid them altogether or deal with them confidently should they occur.

Take a moment and imagine your podcast in a year's time. Envision that it is steadily building a listenership, engaging devoted fans, and providing genuine value to those who tune in. Picture yourself easily navigating production schedules, consistently sticking with your routines, actively refining your format, and proudly standing behind the polished, impactful show you create. That vision isn't wishful thinking. It's a real possibility when you start on this journey armed with the insight provided in this book and a commitment to continuous learning and exploration.

As you move forward, remember that every challenge is an opportunity in disguise. Whether it's perfecting your sound, sharpening your interview skills, or crafting more compelling calls to action, you have the curiosity and willingness to put forth the extra effort that steers your show in the right direction. And it starts here with this small but mighty book. By avoiding these common mistakes, you'll set a solid foundation for a podcast that not only survives, but thrives.

So go ahead, press "record," and trust in your ability to deliver a compelling message. You are now equipped to develop your show with confidence and clarity, and provide your listeners with content that is worthy of their time and loyalty. The next great episode is yours to create and I can't wait to hear how it goes. Please consider rating and reviewing this book so you can share your success with me and other potential podcasters. Now get to work on that first episode...your audience is waiting!

References

Buzzsprout. (n.d.). *Global Podcast Statistics.* Retrieved September 2023, from https://www.buzzsprout.com/global-podcast-stats

Chartable. (n.d.). *Insights & Trends in Podcasting.* Retrieved September 2023, from https://chartable.com/blog

Edison Research. (2023). *The Infinite Dial 2023.* Retrieved from https://www.edisonresearch.com/the-infinite-dial-2023

Interactive Advertising Bureau (IAB). (n.d.). *Podcast Advertising Industry Reports.* Retrieved September 2023, from https://www.iab.com/podcasts/

Nielsen. (n.d.). *Podcasting Today Reports.* Retrieved September 2023, from https://www.nielsen.com/us/en/insights/podcasting/

Pew Research Center. (n.d.). *Audio and Podcasting Research.* Retrieved September 2023, from https://www.pewresearch.org/topics/audio-and-podcasting/

Podcast Insights. (n.d.). *2023 Podcast Statistics & Facts.* Retrieved September 2023, from https://www.podcastinsights.com/podcast-statistics/

The Podcast Host. (n.d.). *Podcasting FAQ & Guides.* Retrieved September 2023, from https://www.thepodcasthost.com/

Podchaser. (n.d.). *Podchaser Insights & Resources.* Retrieved September 2023, from https://www.podchaser.com/articles

Podnews. (n.d.). *Podcast Industry Articles & Analysis.* Retrieved September 2023, from https://podnews.net/article

About the Author

M.N. Osuna is a podcaster, nurse educator, author and online course creator living in Northern California. Her show, *Straight A Nursing*, consistently ranks as the top nursing podcast in the medicine category and has accumulated over 11 million downloads.

www.ingramcontent.com/pod-product-compliance
Lightning Source LLC
LaVergne TN
LVHW010041070326
832903LV00071B/4595